Cornerstones of Freedom

The Story of
MISSISSIPPI STEAMBOATS

By R. Conrad Stein

Illustrated by Tom Dunnington

CHILDRENS PRESS ®

CHICAGO

Library of Congress Cataloging-in-Publication Data

Stein, R. Conrad.
  The story of Mississippi steamboats.

  (Cornerstones of freedom)
  Summary: A brief history of the steamboats which
plied the Mississippi River from the early 1800s until
the beginning of the age of the railroad later in the
century.
  1. River steamers—Mississippi River—History—
Juvenile literature. 2. Mississippi River—Navigation—
History—Juvenile literature. [1. River steamers—
Mississippi River—History. 2. Steamboats—Mississippi
River—History. 3. Mississippi River—Navigation—
History] I. Dunnington, Tom, ill. II. Title.
III. Series.

VM23.S74 1987   386'.22436'0977   86-31753
ISBN 0-516-04726-4

In the 1850s, a steamboat named the *Paul Jones* chugged up the southern Mississippi River. Its passage seemed serene, but as every river pilot knew, below the most peaceful-looking waters lurked fallen trees, jagged rocks, or sandbars. Any one of these hazards could spell doom to a river vessel. It was the job of the pilot to steer his steamboat around these deadly obstacles, even though he could not always see them. The pilot had to know every inch of the mighty Mississippi as if it were the hallway in his own home.

Piloting the *Paul Jones* was a cub pilot—a trainee—alone at the controls for the first time. It was clear daylight and the cub knew this section of the river was free from dangers. But could he be certain?

"My imagination began to construct dangers out of nothing," the cub later wrote. "And they multiplied faster than I could keep the run of them. All at once I imagined I saw shoal water ahead!"

A "shoal" was a giant tree that had tumbled from the bank and lay mired on the bottom; "shoal water" was the peculiar whitecap that broke above the submerged tree. To the cub pilot's horror, the *Paul Jones* bore directly toward the shoal at full speed. The spiked branches of that dead tree could gouge the boat's bottom and sink it.

"I was helpless," wrote the young pilot. "I did not know what in the world to do. I was quaking from head to foot, and I could have hung my hat on my eyes, they stuck out so far." In a panic he darted to the speaker tube and shouted to the engineer below decks, "Oh, Ben, if you love me, *back* her! Quick, Ben! Oh, back the immortal *soul* out of her!"

Then the cub heard deep belly laughs coming from the crew below. He discovered that the captain had conspired with the regular pilot to leave him alone on deck, knowing he would panic and make a fool of himself. The steamboat was in no danger at all.

The cub pilot was Samuel Langhorne Clemens. He recounted this incident in his book *Life on the Mississippi*. Clemens had grown up along the river, and as a boy he fell under the spell of the glamorous Mississippi steamboats. He often watched crewmen measure the river depths by casting overboard rods that were tied to ropes. When the crewman determined the water was two fathoms (twelve feet) deep, he shouted up to the pilot, "Mark twain!" (meaning "Mark two"). Clemens liked the ring. Eventually he became a writer and changed his name; today millions of readers know Mark Twain as a great American author.

The rich lore of the Mississippi steamboat era begins with the river itself. Slicing the country almost in half, the Mississippi begins in northern Minnesota as a stream so small one can wade across it, and ends flowing mightily into the Gulf of Mexico. For centuries, Indian canoeists used the river to carry on trade. The northern tribes called it Mitchisipi or Misipi, meaning "Big River" or "Father of the Waters." French and Spanish explorers later sailed upon this broad river. The French founded the city of New Orleans at its mouth in 1718. Americans started using the river for commerce in the 1790s.

In the days before steam-powered boats, Americans plied the river in either flatboats or keelboats. The simplest form of flatboat was nothing more than a log raft that a pioneer farmer built and floated downriver with his crops piled aboard. When he reached New Orleans the farmer sold his crops, junked the boat, and often walked home. That walk could total one thousand miles. More elaborate flatboats had rudders, oars, and perhaps a small house on top. But the boats were still designed to be discarded at the end of their journey because they could not travel upstream.

Keelboats were able to make their way upstream, but only through the heroic efforts of their crewmen. The average keelboat was sixty to seventy feet long, about eighteen feet wide, and carried a crew of eight to fifteen men. A keelboat run from Pittsburgh on the Ohio River to New Orleans took four to six weeks going downstream. The same trip going upstream took at least four laborious months. To move upriver, keelboat crewmen rowed, jabbed long poles into the river bottom, pushed, tugged, and cursed their bulky vessels into going against the flow of the powerful river.

Flatboats and keelboats operated throughout most of the nineteenth century, but starting in the early 1800s they worked in the shadows of the steamboats. Those glorious craft became queens of the Mississippi.

The world's first commercially successful steamboat was built in 1807 by the brilliant American engineer Robert Fulton. Called the *Clermont*, it carried passengers along the Hudson River in New York. The design was a marriage of a steam engine, a large boat, and a rotating drum of paddle wheels.

Hoping to extend his business, Fulton commissioned another steamboat, the *New Orleans*. It was built in Pittsburgh in 1811, and its maiden run was supposed to take the vessel to the Mississippi River and finally to the city of New Orleans. This trip proved to be one of the most heroic voyages in all of steamboat history.

The *New Orleans* began its bizarre series of adventures at the village of Louisville, Kentucky. There the captain's wife gave birth to a baby. Next, the craft had to run down a stretch of rapids that boatmen swore would wreck it. To steer a steamboat, a pilot had to maintain a speed faster than the water he rode upon, so the *New Orleans* entered the

rapids at full steam. After the craft miraculously survived the rapids, the earth below it suddenly bounced and roared. One of the most severe earthquakes in known history struck the region, tearing down riverbanks, sinking old islands, and raising new ones. The boat's pilot was bewildered by the unfamiliar land he now saw ahead of him.

The very next day the *New Orleans* was pursued by Chickasaw Indians in war canoes. The braves believed the craft had caused the earthquake.

Despite its ordeal, the *New Orleans* reached its destination. It had proved that a steam-powered boat could carry passengers and freight through the Mississippi and its tributaries.

Shortly afterward, businessman Henry Shreve realized the riches that could be made with river steamboats and built a new vessel. Though he was not an engineer, Shreve designed a craft especially for the shallow, snag-ridden Mississippi. His boat sat conspicuously high in the water. He put the engine on top of the main deck and built a second deck over the engine. This design—a raft with an engine on top—was followed by all subsequent riverboat builders. Eventually a third deck appeared. Henry Shreve is generally considered to be the father of the Mississippi steamboat. His boat yard came to be called Shreveport, and it grew into one of Louisiana's leading cities.

About 270 river steamboats were built in the twenty years after the *New Orleans* made its maiden voyage. These vessels were of two basic types—the side-wheelers and the stern-wheelers. The stern-wheelers used one wide paddle wheel at the rear of the boat, while the side-wheelers had two sets of paddle wheels, one along each side. Side-wheelers were favored on the Mississippi because they had two engines. This enabled the pilot to order forward speed on one wheel and reverse on the other, so that the craft could make sharp turns. Stern-wheelers were preferred on the tributaries because they were generally a more narrow craft than the side-wheelers.

There were few settlers along the Mississippi River when the steamboats began operating. At that time, the rest of the country referred to the Mississippi River region as "the West." Steamboats helped to open this western land. Because goods and people could be readily transported, port towns grew along the Mississippi. They included Natchez, Vicksburg, Memphis, and Saint Louis.

As steamboats became more popular with passengers, designers stretched their imaginations to turn bulky paddle wheels and towering chimneys into surprisingly graceful features. They covered the decks with gingerbread designs and painted pictures on the boxes that covered the paddle wheels. People called the steamboats "floating palaces" or "wedding cakes" and compared them to "swans floating on the water."

The interiors were equally splendid. The main cabin served as a dining room and social hall for first-class passengers. Its walls were often lined with oil paintings and gleaming mirrors. Cut-glass chandeliers hung from the ceiling. Steamboat owners readily spent more than a thousand dollars—a fortune at that time—just for carpets. Dinner menus offered ten choices of meats and at least fifteen desserts. The competition to attract first-class passengers was frantic, and rival owners were willing to spend more and more money on luxuries to lure more customers.

Not all Mississippi steamboats were grand passenger vessels. Many were hard-working packets. The packet boats operated on regular, announced runs, and their captains tried to keep them on schedule. In addition to passengers, they carried mail and freight. Their freight included bales of cotton, barrels of sugar and molasses, sacks of rice, and crates of machinery.

The comings and goings of the great steamboats stirred excitement in the riverside towns. Boat whistles could be heard a mile off, and the sound sent townspeople hurrying to the waterfront. The steamboats brought in exotic products, sometimes a tour-

ing theater company, or maybe even a circus. The magic of the boats enthralled the youth of the river towns. "When I was a boy," wrote Mark Twain, "there was but one permanent ambition among my comrades in our village on the west bank of the Mississippi River. That was to be a steamboat man."

The two decades from 1840 to 1860 were the heyday of the steamboat era. By 1850, one thousand steam-powered vessels worked the rivers, and ship-builders could not keep up with new orders. The grand packets reached the height of elegance as boats became larger and designers covered their three decks with fanciful decorations.

But these frills failed to mask the fact that the boats were dangerous for passengers and crew. Few river steamboats died of old age. The average life of a boat was a mere five years: it either sank because of a ripped bottom, succumbed to an accidental fire, or was destroyed when its engine exploded.

Boiler explosions plagued steamboat operations from the earliest days. The boilers held high-pressure steam that was released in spurts to drive the pistons, which in turn rotated the paddle wheels. Most riverboats burned wood to produce steam. Often the red-hot furnaces forced steam pressure beyond what the boilers could hold, resulting in a devastating explosion. Records show that by 1850 at least 185 steamboats had blown up, resulting in the deaths of about fourteen hundred people.

A spectacular explosion ripped the steamer *Louisiana* in 1849 while it was tied up at the levee in New Orleans. The explosion was so powerful it leveled the two boats next to the *Louisiana*. Eighty-six people were reported killed during that tragedy.

The worst disaster ever to take place on the rivers was caused by an explosion. In April 1865, a steamer called the *Sultana* carried home 2,400 Union soldiers who had spent much of the Civil War in Confederate

prison camps. With that many troops crammed aboard, the *Sultana* was overloaded to at least six times its capacity. Near Memphis a boiler blew up and the ship caught fire. It was a pitch-dark night, pouring rain, and the river was at flood stage, making it nearly three miles wide. Also, the soldiers aboard were weak and ill after years of near-starvation prison camp rations. The dead and missing in the *Sultana* wreck totaled 1,547—more than were lost in the *Titanic* disaster of 1912.

Fires caused by carelessness also took their toll of river craft. The wooden boats were tinderboxes, and the tiniest blaze quickly became a roaring inferno. A French visitor named Michael Chevalier, who traveled on riverboats, was shocked at slipshod American safety measures: "The Americans show a singular indifference in regard to fires. They smoke without the least concern in the midst of half-open cotton-bales. . . . They ship gunpowder with no more precaution than if it were . . . maize or salt pork."

Between 1811 and 1850 about four thousand people were killed or injured in steamboat accidents. This dismal record failed to diminish the glamour or the popularity of the magnificent riverboats.

On its river run, a steamboat was entirely in the hands of the pilot. If the pilot wished to dock at an unscheduled port, the captain had to oblige—even if the captain happened to be the boat's owner as well. The pilot's authority was complete because the safety of the valuable boat and its passengers rested on his sharp eye and his keen mind. In day or night, fog or clear, the pilot had to have etched in his memory every slight bend in the river and the location of all its underwater hazards. Mark Twain once wrote, "I haven't got enough brains to be a pilot; and

if I had I wouldn't have strength enough to carry them around, unless I went on crutches."

While the pilot ruled the boat's passage through the river, the captain lorded over every other aspect of the vessel. Quite often he was the owner or at least part owner of the boat. He hired and fired the ship's officers. He charmed the gracious passengers and punished the rowdy ones.

One of the most famous steamboat captains was Tom Leathers, who lived in Natchez. He stood six feet, four inches tall, weighed a muscular 270 pounds, and had blazing red hair and a full beard. He once said, "What's the use of being a steamboat captain if you can't tell the world to go to the devil?" Tom Leathers was known to laugh at danger and allow no man to give him orders—except, of course, the pilot.

Below the captain came the mates and the engineers. At the bottom of the ladder were the roustabouts, who loaded cargo and firewood onto the boat and worked on the decks. Their toil was exhausting and their pay low. To relieve the dreariness of their job the roustabouts often sang. While hauling bales of cotton up the gangplank, their voices lifted in this song:

Now boys, we're on the steamer *Natchez*,
And we got to load this cotton and cottonseed here
Before anybody can shut his eyes like he's sleepy;
So we might just as well tear around.

Riverboat passengers came from all walks of life. Salesmen and dealers in farm products enjoyed the ballrooms and cabins of the grand passenger steamers. Simple farm folk visiting relatives bought low-class tickets on the less celebrated packets. Gambling on card games was popular aboard the boats. But the image that each vessel carried at least one smooth-talking, immaculately-dressed professional gambler is largely an invention of fiction writers. Most captains rudely kicked professional gamblers off their vessels. Still, cardsharps

passing themselves off as salesmen managed to work the boats and cheat the more naive passengers.

Nothing thrilled the riverfront communities more than a steamboat race. Most races were impromptu rather than staged affairs. They occurred when two steamboats headed for the same port were running neck and neck, and suddenly one pilot ordered his engineer to fire up the boilers because he wished to dock first. When a race broke out, word of it traveled up the Mississippi even faster than the speeding vessels. People in the sleepy waterfront towns rushed to the levee to watch the dueling monsters and place bets on the outcome.

Racing these powerful vessels, whose boilers were prone to blowing up when overheated, was a risky game. Insurance companies berated captains for engaging in such sport. Nevertheless, the races went on. The grandest race of all took place after the Civil War, when the age of Mississippi steamboats was entering its decline.

In 1869, Captain Tom Leathers built his sixth boat, the *Natchez*. It was as long as a New Orleans city block, was driven by giant paddle wheels forty-three feet in diameter, and was powered by a high-pressure steam engine that produced two thousand horsepower. (By contrast, the 1811 *New Orleans* mustered only one hundred horsepower.) The *Natchez*'s major rival on the Mississippi was the *Robert E. Lee*, another elegant passenger boat with a reputation for speed.

By chance, the two boats were in New Orleans together in June 1870, and both were scheduled for runs to Saint Louis. With great fanfare, Captain Leathers announced that the *Natchez* would depart New Orleans at the same time as the *Robert E. Lee*. Word of this challenge was sent by telegraph, and the entire Mississippi buzzed with excitement. News of the contest was even clicked to Europe on the transatlantic cable. Undoubtedly, the *Natchez* versus the *Robert E. Lee* was the most exciting race ever held on the Mississippi. But the contest ended in controversy. The captain of the *Robert E. Lee* stripped his boat of cargo and arranged to refuel in midstream. Tom Leathers considered such procedures to be "unsporting" and sailed as he would on a normal run. The *Robert E. Lee* finished first, but supporters of the *Natchez* cried foul and refused to honor their bets.

By the late 1870s, the grand river packets were losing a race against time. When the boats began their operations, the Mississippi River valley was thought of as "the West." But by the time the Civil War was over, the West had become a far-flung frontier more than a thousand miles beyond the river. The new lands of the growing country were served best by railroads. As railroad tracks spanned the great river and snaked along its banks, the paddle-wheel steamers fell slowly into disuse. Certainly some paddle wheelers worked as freighters even into the 1950s, but the glory days for Mississippi steamboats ended with the age of the railroad.

Nevertheless, the memory of the steamers lived on in poetry, story, and song. They were a useful and oddly beautiful craft that both inspired and served a pioneer people. To the settlers along the Mississippi, the boats embodied all the richness and beauty of their growing nation. No wonder, then, that the beloved steamboats found their way into sentimental songs like this:

> She's on her way to New Orleans!
> Good-bye, my lover, good-bye!
> She's bound to pass the *Robert E. Lee*,
> Good-bye, my lover, good-bye!
> Oh, let her go by!

About the Author

R. Conrad Stein was born and grew up in Chicago. He enlisted in the Marine Corps at the age of eighteen and served for three years. He then attended the University of Illinois where he received a bachelor's degree in history. He later studied in Mexico, earning an advanced degree from the University of Guanajuato. Mr. Stein is the author of many other books, articles, and short stories written for young people.

Mr. Stein now lives in Chicago with his wife, Deborah Kent, who is also a writer of books for young readers, and their daughter Janna.

About the Artist

Tom Dunnington hails from the Midwest, having lived in Minnesota, Iowa, Illinois, and Indiana. He attended the John Herron Institute of Art in Indianapolis and the American Academy of Art and the Chicago Art Institute in Chicago. He has been an art instructor and illustrator for many years. In addition to illustrating books, Mr. Dunnington is working on a series of paintings of endangered birds (produced as limited edition prints). His current residence is in Oak Park, Illinois, where he works as a free-lance illustrator and is active in church and community youth work.